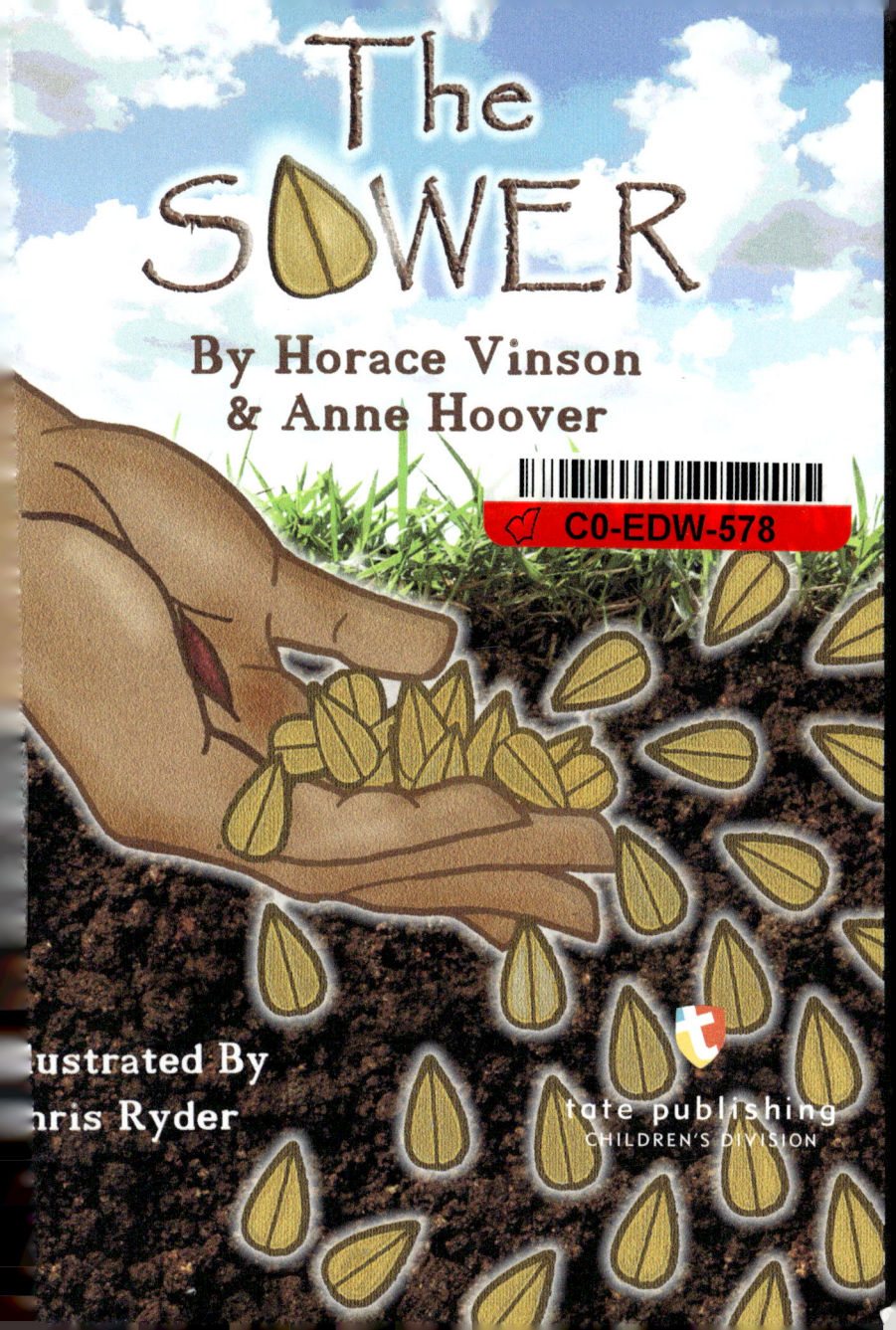

The Sower
Copyright © 2016 by Horace Vinson & Anne Hoover. All rights reserved.

This title is also available as a Tate Out Loud product. Visit www.tatepublishing.com for more information.

No part of this publication may be reproduced, stored in a retrieval system or transmitted in any way by any means, electronic, mechanical, photocopy, recording or otherwise without the prior permission of the author except as provided by USA copyright law.

The opinions expressed by the author are not necessarily those of Tate Publishing, LLC.

This novel is a work of fiction. Names, descriptions, entities, and incidents included in the story are products of the author's imagination. Any resemblance to actual persons, events, and entities is entirely coincidental.

Published by Tate Publishing & Enterprises, LLC
127 E. Trade Center Terrace | Mustang, Oklahoma 73064 USA
1.888.361.9473 | www.tatepublishing.com

Tate Publishing is committed to excellence in the publishing industry. The company reflects the philosophy established by the founders, based on Psalm 68:11, "The Lord gave the word and great was the company of those who published it."

Book design copyright © 2016 by Tate Publishing, LLC. All rights reserved.
Cover and interior design by Chris Ryder, Eileen Cueno
Illustrations by Chris Ryder

Published in the United States of America

ISBN: 978-1-68352-342-0
1. Juvenile Nonfiction / Religion / Bible Stories / New Testament
2. Juvenile Nonfiction / Poetry / General
16.08.31

To my wife and children

who are a precious gift from the Lord

And to my inspiration

my Lord and Savior Jesus Christ

Hello! My name is Immanuel,

And I always serve my Father well!

I rise and shine and put on my shoes,

For I have a special job to do.

My job is to tend to my Father's land,

And I love to fulfill my Father's plan!

Each day I go to my Father and say,

"Abba! What shall I do today?"

In His mighty voice He says to me,

"I want you to plant My special seeds."

So out I go to sow His seeds,

And I pray that they grow to be beautiful trees.

So I throw some here,

and I throw some there.

I spread the special seeds everywhere.

I start out hopeful every day,

Till I notice some seeds that fall by the way.

The birds swoop down, and one by one

They gobble them up until all are gone.

Those seeds will never be fruitful trees,

But I've sown many more seeds than these.

So I throw some more here,

and I throw some more there.

I spread the special seeds everywhere.

I always have fun on my planting walks

Till I notice some seeds that fall on the rocks.

Their roots are too shallow; the sun climbs high,

And without good, deep soil, they wither and die.

Those seeds will never be fruitful trees,

But I've sown many more seeds than these.

So I throw some more here,

and I throw some more there.

I spread the special seeds everywhere.

I find myself having a grand ol' time,

Till I notice some weeds beginning to climb.

The thorns grow fast and choke each plant.

Although it wants to grow, it can't.

Those seeds will never be fruitful trees,

But I've sown in hope more seeds than these.

So I toss some more here,

and I toss some more there.

I spread the special seeds everywhere.

Will my Father's fields ever have beautiful trees,

Full of fruit and birds and bees?

Will His seeds fall lifeless wherever I roam?

Should I keep on planting or just go back home?

But I love my Father, who told me to go.

I will sow and sow until something good grows.

And then...

My job has been tough, but this time around,

Some of my seed falls on good, dark ground.

The seeds sink in and begin to sprout.

Then trunks and branches and leaves spring out!

Before I can blink, the fields are filled!

I know that my Father will be so thrilled!

And now, when I look at the trees, I know

That I plant the seeds, but He makes them grow.

The fruit from each tree will give us more seeds

For me to plant as my Father leads.

My Father's the Grower of all good things.

I can't wait to see what tomorrow will bring!

THE END

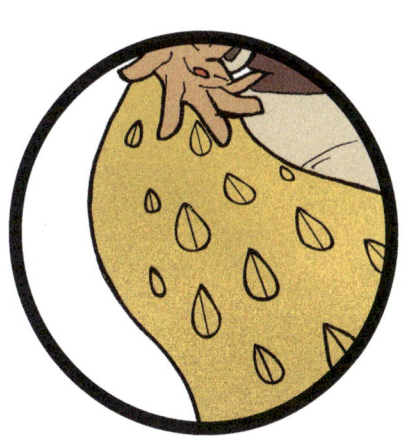

listen|imagine|view|experience

AUDIO BOOK DOWNLOAD INCLUDED WITH THIS BOOK!

In your hands you hold a complete digital entertainment package. In addition to the paper version, you receive a free download of the audio version of this book. Simply use the code listed below when visiting our website. Once downloaded to your computer, you can listen to the book through your computer's speakers, burn it to an audio CD or save the file to your portable music device (such as Apple's popular iPod) and listen on the go!

How to get your free audio book digital download:

1. Visit www.tatepublishing.com and click on the e|LIVE logo on the home page.
2. Enter the following coupon code:
   2149-347b-af19-6b46-0776-a239-583c-c183
3. Download the audio book from your e|LIVE digital locker and begin enjoying your new digital entertainment package today!

CPSIA information can be obtained
at www.ICGtesting.com
Printed in the USA
BVOW07s1145231016
465518BV00015B/10/P